MW01027643

# THE DOORKEEPER

# THE DOORKEEPER:

# IN THE KING'S PRESENCE

By Sandi Funkhouser

Three Sisters Communication, LLC.

Star, Idaho

All biblical quotations are taken from the New International Version of the Bible unless otherwise indicated.

First edition published in 2005.

ISBN 0-9771204-0-6 print ed.
ISBN 0-9771204-1-4 PDF ed.
ISBN 0-9771204-2-2 audio ed.

Cover design by Kari May, True Communications

Funkhouser, Sandi
    The DoorKeeper: In the King's Presence/ Sandi Funkhouser—1st edition.

TO:

OUR KING

# TABLE OF CONTENTS

# Preface

I am not a theologian. I don't even play one on TV. I am simply a fellow traveler on our journey through this life to the next.

The Doorkeeper is my attempt to put into word pictures the many ways I have experienced my heavenly Father's love as He has led me on this journey of discovery. The Doorkeeper is a compilation of vignettes depicting the throne room as each of us—fellow travelers—comes into the presence of God—the King. We may enter the throne room walking up a mountain trail, sitting in a church pew, kneeling at an altar, or mopping the kitchen floor. It happens when our heart opens to His.

I would love to reveal to you the essence of God through this work. However, I can only share the glimpse of His infinite being I have seen and experienced. Each new experience has propelled me a step further down the path of discovery toward God, Himself.

As you read these stories, don't strive to understand some deep truth. Relax, let the story percolate in your spirit, and enjoy what you discover.

Wishing you great joy in your journey,

*Sandi*

# ACKNOWLEDGMENTS

This tiny book has taken years to complete and would not be in your hands now were it not for the encouragement and expertise of many, many precious people.

To my sister, Barb: Thank you for believing in me, in the worth of The Doorkeeper, and for never letting me give up.

To my dear friend, Lois: Thank you for your honest input and constant encouragement.

To my friend and fellow-writer, Gene W.: Thank you for your amazing support and words of wisdom.

To my long-time friend (I never say "old friend" anymore!) and editor, Sandy G.: Thank you for the many hours you spent making my ragged thoughts become polished, powerful images.

To my talented, generous friend, Kathy E: Thank you for the hours of proofing and typesetting given so freely.

To the host of friends who have been my cheerleaders along the way: Thank you for your undying support.

To my children: Thank you for loving me, warts and all, you have been the wind beneath my wings.

To my husband, Allen: Thank you for being my biggest fan and for creating the space for me to bring this to completion.

To my wonderful Lord, who is the object of my love, the source of my life, and the truth behind my words—I bow.

# NEW POSTING

My entire life had built to this moment. For as long as I could remember I held on to one dream—to serve in the position closest to the King. This was the pinnacle of my career. Having served on the front lines, in the trenches, in the most remote parts of the realm, in support of captains and generals, in extreme conditions and at ease, at last my dream was coming true. Today, I would become Doorkeeper in the throne room of the King.

My friends in the barracks wished me well. I think my commander was almost as proud as I was. And my mother, well, she was beside herself—her son, Doorkeeper to the King—who would have ever dreamed of such a thing?

I expected rigorous training, warning about intruders and other dangers, and instruction in palace etiquette. It surprised me when my entire orientation consisted of a fitting for my new royal uniform. In fact, the only official training came when I met my captain. Cap was a brusque yet fatherly man. Slightly shorter than I with a body as solid as concrete, his battle scars were proof of his years as a warrior. But, his eyes drew me in. They were alert, aware and confident yet kind—eyes that had seen it all but ready for surprises, as well. Cap was what we called in the service "seasoned." His only instructions to me were, "Son, nothing can prepare you for the throne room, just follow my lead." With those words, duty called, and he was off down the corridor.

Finally, outfitted in my new uniform—the sash around my middle perfectly centered, boots polished until I could see my dress sword in them, gold brocade properly draped on my shoulder—and my heart beating so loudly it was all I could hear, I was ready. The trumpet for the changing of the guard sounded. It was time.

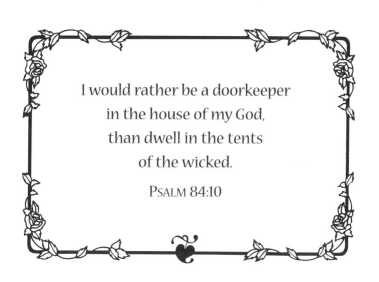

I would rather be a doorkeeper
in the house of my God,
than dwell in the tents
of the wicked.

PSALM 84:10

# Run In

It was my first hour at "the doors." I stood proud and tall just inside the huge, solid-gold doors leading to the King's court. Years of service had taught me just how to cover the knocking of my knees and trembling of my hands as I was overwhelmed by the realization that I was actually here in the King's presence.

Court was in session. The King, sitting on His massive throne was hearing the petitions of powerful dignitaries from throughout the realm. I was feeling the heady responsibility of my new position and tried not to gawk as men whose prowess I had admired for decades strode past me and bowed before the King.

As two particularly honored statesmen began their impassioned pleas, I listened intently. Engrossed in their debate, I jumped at the sound of footsteps running toward the double doors. Bursting through, a little girl raced past, barefoot, braids askew, dress mud-spattered, her hands cupped around something (a feathered friend, if the bits of wing and beak peeking through her fingers were any indication). I lunged to catch the waif but missed. Panicked, I noticed Cap's amusement. With a wink, he nodded for me to look toward the King.

As the little bare feet slapping against the polished marble floor ran straight toward the throne, I was confused. Why wasn't Cap worried? Why was she allowed to interrupt the business of the kingdom? Afraid I had missed a cue, I looked toward the King and my fears dissolved. As she ran up the stairs straight to the throne, my mighty King, a look of delight on His face, reached down and lifted the child onto His knee. While the court watched and waited, she whispered in the King's ear. He nodded gravely and tenderly opened her grubby fingers to reveal a tiny, wounded bird.

With unhurried care, His Majesty placed the creature in His handkerchief, set its wing, and dried the little girl's tears. Together, they gently stroked the bird until its quivering stopped, as did the child's, and it settled into a healing sleep. The King whispered in the child's ear and kissed her cheek. She threw her arms around His neck in an adoring hug and skipped back through the huge doors, cradling the tiny bird in the King's handkerchief.

Bewildered, I looked to Cap, who mouthed the answer to my unspoken question, "The King's daughter."

Let us then approach the throne of grace with confidence, so that we may receive mercy and find grace to help in our time of need.

HEBREWS 4:16

# DEETER

I was peacefully enjoying the wonders of the throne room when trumpets sounded the arrival of nobility. Pulling myself to full attention and fixing my salute, I opened the grand doors with a flourish. Looking for the dignitary, I hardly noticed the old woman in a musty gray-black coat, her gnarled fingers wrapped around a tattered Bible, as she shuffled feebly through the doors toward the King.

No one else entered. Thinking I had missed someone extremely important, I looked frantically to Cap for direction. Cap, veteran of the throne room, nodded towards the bent figure slowly but deliberately plodding towards the throne and signaled that I should simply watch.

Halfway to the King, the old woman was suddenly bathed in an infusion of light that seemed to penetrate rather than illuminate her. As the light intensified, I became aware of two simultaneous occurrences. The ancient woman was singing songs of love and adoration for the King as a transformation began.

Her bent spine straightened and her wretched, shabby coat evaporated as a shining white robe covered the now tall, strong body. Her once arthritic fingers were now wrapped around the handle of an enormous sword, razor sharp on both edges, which she swung with ease in a salute to the palace guard and then to the King.

She bowed in worship, then towering above the nobles and statesmen, raised her beautiful head and declared, "I have come as you requested, My King."

A planning session followed as the King outlined His strategy for an upcoming battle in which she was to be the principal champion for the realm. The woman nodded confidently as the King outlined her assignments. When the meeting was over, she bowed her head and the King laid His hands on her shoulders, blessed her with the promise of His presence, embraced her, and sent her on her mission.

Awestruck, I could only stare as the towering figure approached the grand doors. The light began to diminish; the sword again became a tattered Bible. As she neared me, I saw her hands curl back to their gnarled positions around the Bible, her shoulders hunch, and her back bend forward. The warrior's stride became a shuffle and she looked to me for help as the huge double doors loomed in front of her.

Leaping to open the doors and offering an

assisting hand under the old saint's elbow, I was delighted to look into the eyes of the dear soul and meet the clear, courageous gaze of a warrior.

I watched until the bent form, still humming love songs, disappeared from view, then turned to my mentor seeking explanation once again.

"That is Deeter," Cap explained, "one of the King's champions. You will see a lot of her. She comes whenever the King calls, and He calls her often." And again I wondered at what I had seen.

Not by might, nor by power,
but by my Spirit,
says the Lord Almighty.

Zechariah 4:6b

## COMING HOME

Occasionally, the King excused Himself from the statesmen and warriors, nobles and musicians, and walked to the great doors. I loved these times—so close to the King I could feel the whoosh of His robes. His nearness lifted my spirits. But, the look on the King's face as He stood looking down the outer path that led to the throne room troubled me. Such longing filled the King's eyes. I thought perhaps if I worshipped more heartily the King would be comforted. As the day wore on, however, His look of longing intensified.

I was about to ask Cap if the King always did this and if there was anything we could do when a repugnant odor filtered through the doorway. Pigs!!

Curious, I stepped outside to find the source of the smell. At first, I could not see any activity. As my eyes adjusted and I began to look into the dusky areas beyond the light of the path, the dim forms of people emerged in the shadows. They were working listlessly. Even from a distance, I could see that their tattered and dirty clothing hung loosely on their emaciated frames. Their shoulders sagged and their movements were lethargic. I could not see their eyes, but their whole demeanor spoke of hopelessness. And each was alone—achingly, desperately, unbearably—alone.

As I watched, one of them dropped his shovel and slowly raised his head. His shoulders lifted ever so slightly, and he turned toward the light which shone down the path from the open doors of the throne room. One halting step at a time, he began to make his way to the path. None of the others looked up as he passed; they remained alone in their misery.

The man's shoulders began to slump once more and he stood still, uncertain. I held my breath willing him to continue. His feet did not move, but his body seemed to vacillate between continuing toward the light and returning to the misery behind him. His head shook back and forth; then, the struggle evidently settled, the man stepped onto the path.

As soon as the poor soul came clearly into view, I knew where the rancid smell of pigs had originated. Ugh! I also noticed that the man's tattered clothing had obviously been royal robes. The man's lined and sunburned face was cultured and regal, and his hands, now scarred and callused, looked as if they had belonged to a musician. Yet now, he was covered with the filth of a pig sty. The man's eyes met mine full of humiliation, shame, and utter desperation.

Footsteps behind me caught my attention. I turned to see the King running towards me. Never had I seen the King run! I froze. But the King's eyes were aglow with unimaginable delight and fixed upon the decrepit man still far down the path.

Before the King could reach him, the man fell to the ground sobbing, "No, Daddy, don't touch me. I am ..." His words were cut short as the King swept him into His embrace and shouted with uproarious joy, "My son has come home!"

By the time the King and His son reached me at the grand doors, the stench was gone, a new robe covered the man's shoulders, and all evidence of filth had been washed away. As the King and son entered the throne room, the King placed His ring on His son's finger.

The son, no longer alone, his regal posture restored, caught my eye to nod his thanks as he passed, and this time I saw in those eyes humility, gratitude, and peace.

Then the celebration began!

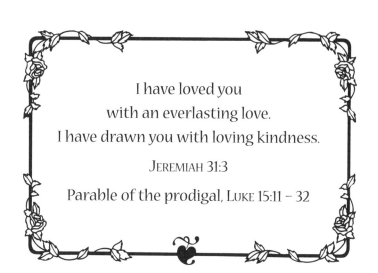

I have loved you
with an everlasting love.
I have drawn you with loving kindness.

JEREMIAH 31:3

Parable of the prodigal, LUKE 15:11 – 32

# BEARING GIFTS

A faint tinkling caught my ear. Peering out the doors and down the path, I saw a man coming toward me. As he walked, the man juggled the load he carried. He wore an oversized pack from which dangled fine silver ornaments, goblets, and jewelry. His clothing was elegant, from his ornately embroidered golden vest and silk shirt to the expensive fabric of his trousers and his highly polished boots. He wore two beautiful rings, and in his arms he carried lavishly wrapped packages, which seemed to be quite heavy. He constantly adjusted the load often swooping to catch a slipping package.

He was humming as he made his way toward the double doors. Yet, I noticed the man's eyes were haggard, and the load he carried became more unmanageable with every step.

Just then the packages in the good man's arms began to cascade to the ground. I leaped to catch the tumbling pile, but several packages eluded me. The pilgrim's face crumbled in disappointment as I helped him gather up the battered presents.

"Ruined. Ruined. Ruined," moaned the man. "All my precious gifts ruined," he lamented as he unsuccessfully attempted to straighten the tattered bows and uncrumple the dented corners on the gold-wrapped boxes. "I've worked so long and come so far. They were perfect. My whole life spent preparing for this day, and now this." Tears streamed down his cheeks.

As the poor pilgrim bemoaned his loss, the King's little daughter ran by, still a bit mud-splattered, still barefoot, hair flying. This time I grinned as she darted through the great hall straight to the throne. The pilgrim's jaw fell open, and he nearly dropped his packages as he watched her give the King a huge hug and wet kiss on His cheek, which He returned with equal enthusiasm. His Majesty listened intently as she shared with Him her newest delight. Then, with a smile and a wave she jumped down and was off, out the doors and down the path on her way to new discoveries.

The pilgrim sputtered, "But, but, but…she was muddy. She was so undignified. She was untidy. How could she just run in like that? I've prepared all my life to approach the King!" The pilgrim's emotions spilled out in a mixture of amazement and indignation. He continued to mutter as he worked with his load.

I started to explain about the King's daughter, when the pilgrim stopped and stood absolutely still. A little light began to glisten in his eyes.

"He hugged her," the pilgrim whispered as he

walked toward the throne, forgetting several packages still lying alongside the path.

"She whispered in His ear," I heard him mutter as he passed me, not even noticing the gifts I had gathered and held out to him.

"He listened," the pilgrim continued to himself, the light now glowing on his face. He quickened his pace and fastened his eyes on the throne.

As if realizing the load was slowing him down, the pilgrim dropped the gifts in his arms and shrugged out of his heavy pack. "He loves her," he declared loudly. "He loves ME!" he shouted. With golden vest flapping and legs churning, he ran straight into the arms of the King. Secure, he looked into the eyes of His Father and began to share his new discoveries with Him.

I was chuckling to myself as I deposited the pilgrim's discarded gifts outside the doors, dragging the enormous pack out as well.

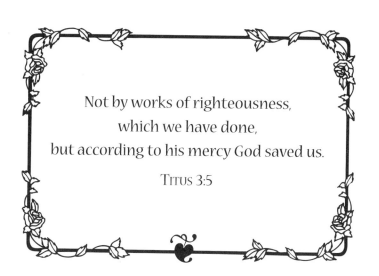

Not by works of righteousness,
which we have done,
but according to his mercy God saved us.

TITUS 3:5

# ANGRY

I was keeping one eye on the activities near the throne, but my attention was drawn to a conversation being held just outside the grand doors. I could only catch snippets of what sounded like an argument.

"Why go in there? It's His fault!"

"I'm not going to stay, I'm just going to tell Him what I…."

"…not go in at all…."

"Serve Him right…."

Back and forth the words flew. I was now thoroughly engrossed in the drama. Before I could determine whether this was truly a conversation or a monologue, a demanding "thud, thud, thud" reverberated through the doors.

Swinging them open, I found myself nose-to-nose with a contorted face. Blinking, I took in the rage-filled eyes, reddened cheeks, bulging veins, and gasping sobs nearing hysteria. On the alert, I stood my ground and looked to Cap, who turned to the King. At the King's nod, I stepped to one side and warily let the "hostile" through.

Once in the throne room, the traveler, a woman, did an about-face, obviously intent on leaving; however, I had already closed the doors. A struggle with indecision warred on her face, then she turned back toward the throne.

Suddenly, a torrent of pent-up fury surged through the woman, propelling her forward. Enraged eyes popping, she tore toward the King, stopping at the foot of the stairs. Rigidly, she stood before Him with hands clenched and shoulders tensed nearly to her ears, the waves of emotion nearly visible as her chest heaved.

Shaking her fist in the King's face, she shouted, "This is NOT what you promised! What did I do to deserve THIS? What more do you want? You're a fraud! Why…"

Before the irate woman could finish, the King rose from His throne, walked down the stairs and stood facing her. I was focused on the King's eyes because as I looked, I saw the image of the enraged woman reflected in them. Yet, instead of rage, I encountered raw agony, in place of accusation, I saw confusion, and rather than rejection, I read fear. The woman dove at the King, fists flying, angry invectives spewing. Unruffled and compassionate, the King enfolded the woman in His arms. He held her tightly until the blows slowed and the shouting became broken-hearted sobbing, then quiet weeping. For some time, the King simply held the woman nestled against His shoulder just as He had His daughter,

Finally, with infinite tenderness, the King said, "Come," and drew the broken traveler to the edge of the gallery. The entire realm was visible from this viewpoint.

Everyone in the throne room watched as the King pointed to the past, from which the traveler had come. Her shoulders bunched as if in pain and tears slid down her cheeks. Then the King turned the woman around and pointed in the opposite direction—the future. As her eyes followed the King's gesture, they widened and a light of understanding began to glow in them. Her face streaming with tears now, she knelt and worshipped.

Without realizing it, my hand had fastened on my sword. I felt the tension release as I relaxed my grip. It would be okay. The traveler's countenance became serene. Pain still etched her face, but the pulsating anger was gone.

After a final embrace from the King, the woman turned and quietly walked toward the doors. She paused to rest a while against the far wall. When she felt ready, she turned and silently slipped out the doors.

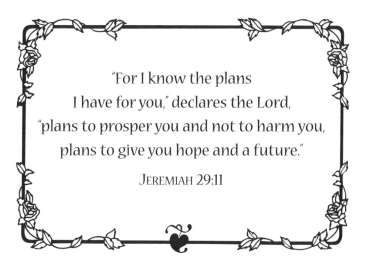

"For I know the plans
I have for you," declares the Lord,
"plans to prosper you and not to harm you,
plans to give you hope and a future."

JEREMIAH 29:11

# THE RUNNER

The panorama from the throne room was as full and clear as the view from a mountaintop on a pristine day. I was fascinated to find that, rather than being limited to four walls, the King's throne and gallery overlooked His entire realm. Events in every corner of the kingdom could be seen as clearly as if they were taking place in the throne room itself.

In the few hours I had been at my post, I noticed also that those in the gallery were not only spectators; they seemed completely consumed with the scenes playing out before them. They were observing, yet, their faces showed their empathy with the pilgrims battling, struggling, conquering, and rejoicing throughout the King's domain; it was as if they were adding their strength to each one they watched.

I was pondering this when the gallery began to cheer, rooting for someone somewhere, urging them on. Someone was approaching. I could hear them faintly. Opening both great doors, I saw what looked like a frail, stooped elderly woman far down the path mumbling to herself and shuffling toward the doorway. As the roar of the crowd reached her, however, something changed! Her head came up and she began to run. Her stride lengthened to a practiced lope; the watery eyes became alight with anticipation. I heard her labored breath become the steady panting of a runner as she raced closer to the grand doors. As she passed through, the cheering erupted into a thunderous ovation.

Now, with each stride, the runner seemed to gain strength. Her body glistened with sweat. And then, she saw the throne and the King waiting with a laurel crown in His hands.

Her eyes locked on the King and the weariness of a lifetime spent training, running, striving toward this moment fell away. The runner's feet seemed to fly inches above the marble floor; her spent body took on the beauty and grace of a gazelle. She took no notice of the path before her, nor the burning in every muscle, nor the pain of every breath. Neither did she hear the cheering crescendo as she passed the stands. Hers arms were reaching, her whole being was focused on the King, the crown...the finish.

The shouts of the crowd took on an invigorating cadence, and the runner's pace increased to an all-out sprint. Her face radiated with sheer, undiluted joy as she covered the last meters of her race. Upon reaching her King—as exultant pandemonium broke out in the gallery—she threw herself, panting, spent, triumphant at His feet.

It was then that I realized the King Himself had been leading the cheering! He placed the laurel crown on the runner's head, and lifting her to her feet, declared with booming delight, "Well done thou good and faithful servant. Enter into the joy of the LORD!"

I glanced sideways at Cap, and knew from the look on his face, we shared the same thought. There was no place in all the realm we would rather be than in the doorway of the throne room at this moment!

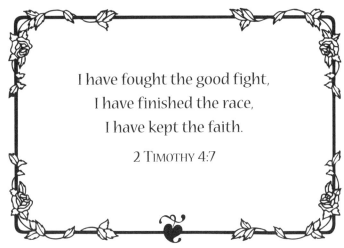

I have fought the good fight,
I have finished the race,
I have kept the faith.

2 TIMOTHY 4:7

# RESCUE

I had served my King for eons, but never had I held a post that fulfilled me to the core as this one did.

Incense drifted into the throne room filling it with a cloud of fragrance. The aromas from throughout the kingdom were as different as the regions from which they came, yet they never seemed to clash. I was aware that these fragrances were evidence of people in the realm praying. It was interesting to me that the intensity of the fragrances directly affected the number of royal troops present to do the King's bidding. As the fragrant cloud increased, the King called more troops to His throne. When it diminished, their numbers dwindled. When the cloud grew thick, I experienced a kind of headiness to the point of feeling almost giddy. The power in the throne room pulsated at such times.

As the fragrances swirled, a crescendo of music rose to unbelievable heights of melody, harmony, and beauty—rich expressions of joy and adoration of the King. Worship was always rising to the King, but at times it rose to pinnacles that were pure ecstasy. The angels added their deep voices, and my spirit soared.

I was engulfed in one of these moments of highest worship, aware of nothing but the praise, engulfed in the fragrances of people praying, surrounded by the hosts of heaven summoned to the throne room, when the King suddenly leaped to His feet and commanded, "Silence!"

Startled, I snapped back to duty. A feeble voice floated into the throne room, barely audible, yet recognized by the King even in the midst of the thunderous praise, "Father, help me..." The voice stopped.

46

With a roar, the King issued commands to His troops. The throne room was at attention as His orders rang out. The earth began to quake. Warriors, swords drawn, flew towards the little voice. The King's command was clear, "Rescue my child, NOW!!"

Peering in the direction from which I had heard the voice, I saw the debris of battle. Broken swords and slashed shields littered the scene around one of the King's children: a solitary, valiant, wounded soldier. He had put up a tremendous fight.

The King raised His own sword. With a mighty swipe that seemed to slash through time, space, heaven and earth straight to where the weary soldier struggled to survive, He severed the chains an enemy had begun to wrap around His child. The chains fell off and the enemy warriors fled with the King's hosts in militant pursuit.

Exhausted, the courageous soldier slumped to the floor. The King knelt beside him, wrapped His arms around him, tenderly healing his wounds and soothing his spirit.

It wasn't long before I noticed the incense rising again. The songs of highest worship and victory flooded the throne room, led by the praise coming from the child of the King who had been rescued by his ever-vigilant, mighty Heavenly Father.

Full of joy, I gave myself over to worship. I could not adequately express the wonders I had experienced that day in the throne room of the King.

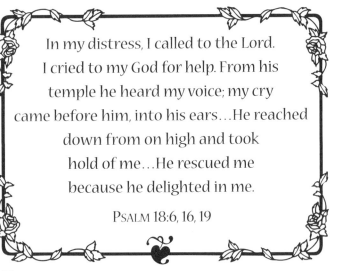

In my distress, I called to the Lord. I cried to my God for help. From his temple he heard my voice; my cry came before him, into his ears…He reached down from on high and took hold of me…He rescued me because he delighted in me.

PSALM 18:6, 16, 19

# THE FISHERMAN

As I manned my post, all my senses heightened. The air pulsated with fragrances, sounds, and movement indescribable in any other realm. I took a moment to savor the brilliance of all I was feeling and drew a deep breath, but nearly choked as a pungent odor assaulted my senses. Fish! Freshly caught, straight from the sea, strident but not rank. Not unpleasant, but definitely not a royal odor. The smell began overcoming the pleasant fruit-like fragrances of the throne room, and I moved to close the doors. "Hold up there, young man!" a voice bellowed at me.

I scanned the path. Striding toward me, one burly

arm draped around the shoulder of a bedraggled, slightly odiferous but happy-looking hoodlum, was a fisherman. His forearms were huge and his gait exhibited the agility of a man used to the rolling of a ship amid tossing waves. His eyes were clear and confident, accented by a twinkle that made it seem as if he would laugh out loud at any moment. His face beamed with the delight of a great catch. The closer the pair came to the throne room the more exuberant they became. By the time they reached the doors, they were fairly dancing.

"Aha, my fine doorkeeper! I have brought a surprise for my King." A tickle of happiness played at my throat and, as I opened the doors wide for the huge man to pass, a chuckle escaped me. I couldn't help it—the fisherman's cheerfulness was contagious.

Once in the King's presence, reverence overcame the fisherman and the merry hoodlum. Slowing their step and dropping to one knee, they bowed. When they looked up, the King stepped down from the throne with arms open wide to meet them. "This is Hugh," the fisherman said to the King.

"I know him well," came the reply, "Just today, I watched as he gave you quite a fight before you reeled him in."

"Yes, there was a battle for this one," the fisherman agreed. "But, we won and he is ready to join you, my King."

"Well done, my friend, well done," cried the King. He embraced the fisherman in a hug befitting his enormity, then turned to welcome Hugh to the kingdom.

A grand celebration commenced, and I was a surprised to see the fisherman turning to leave. "Won't you stay for the celebration?" I asked.

"Nay, nay. Hugh is in good hands now and there are so many more to bring in. Nay, I'll celebrate as I go back to my ocean. It's what I do, you know." With that, the fisherman, still smelling of fish and the sea, strode out the doors and down the path with a lilt in his step and a twinkle in his eye while the celebration continued behind him. I found myself grinning as I swung the doors closed.

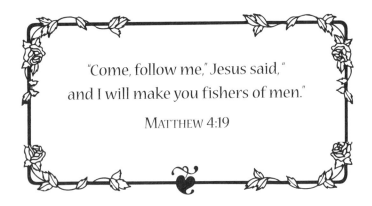

"Come, follow me," Jesus said, "
and I will make you fishers of men."

MATTHEW 4:19

# BURDENED

Heavy footsteps were approaching. From the deliberate clump, clump, clump, I expected to find a tall, hefty man in the doorway. When I opened the doors (to a less than powerful tap) I almost tripped over the demure, almost frail, middle-aged woman. The cause of those heavy footsteps was instantly obvious. On the traveler's back was a huge, ragged, leather pack full of large, ugly stones.

Her breath was coming in short gasps, as she panted (it was the pack that drew attention rather than the woman), "Oh, thank you. Those doors seemed so large and impossible." I gave her my most welcoming smile and showed her in to the hall. As she stepped through the door, I reached to relieve her of her load. But, when I began to lift the burden, she spun around at me, horror-stricken and defensive.

"What are you doing? This is my pack. I've carried it this far myself, and I'll keep it with me now!"

I was taken aback and let her pass, unaided. I didn't know what to think as I watched the woman continue her laborious trek toward the throne. The closer she came to the King, the heavier the rocks in her pack became. Her pace slowed. Her breathing came in great gulps. She sank to the floor in a duck-like walk under her enormous burden. Her eyes grew wild with desperation. Although many servants offered to help her, she vehemently refused. One excruciating step at a time, she labored toward the King.

The business of the throne room continued.

Worshippers worshipped. Dancers danced. Statesmen conducted affairs of state. Warriors prepared and left for battle while others returned with their reports. And still, the weary woman continued her determined journey to the throne, doggedly refusing any aid.

Finally, she could walk no further and I wanted to reach out to her as she slipped to her hands and knees, still moving ever-so-slowly, but I couldn't help her. In moments, her progress stopped completely. Absolutely exhausted, she looked up at the King, still more than half the length of the throne room away and, in a defeated whisper moaned, "I can't…carry…this burden…anymore."

In an instant, the King Himself was down the steps and standing before her. Looking tenderly into her eyes, He carefully slipped the pack off her back. Seeing her panic, He soothed, "I will carry this," and slipped the pack over His own shoulders. Holding her hands in His, He lifted her gently to her feet. She stood before the King, but her shoulders remained bowed, as if she still carried the weight of the pack. With a gentle touch of His finger to her chin, He encouraged her to stand up fully and look directly at Him. Then, He motioned for her to inspect the pack. It was empty!

Radiant is the only word I can think of to describe her expression as the traveler looked from the King, to the pack, and back to the King again. She began to dance, a light, exuberant dance of freedom. The King chuckled and clapped His hands, and I returned to listening for the next footstep on the path.

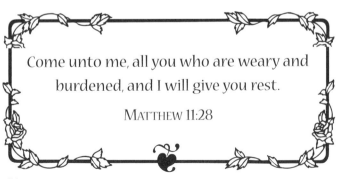

Come unto me, all you who are weary and burdened, and I will give you rest.

MATTHEW 11:28

# REST AND
# REFRESHING

Worship swirled in the
throne room. Songs of
infinite harmony and indescribable melody swirled in
celebration and praise to the King. Joy was rampant.
As the drums played and the flutes trilled and the
stringed instruments resonated, dance broke out
across the room. It was a glorious moment.

In the midst of the celebration, I heard the strong,
measured cadence of a soldier marching toward the
doors. As was my habit by now, I reached to swing
the doors when they burst open and I found myself
face-to-face with a giant, young soldier. His muscles
rippled as he saluted me stiffly and announced with

a voice like a foghorn, "Reporting for R & R, sir."

"R & R?" I wondered out loud.

"Rest and refreshing, sir," explained the soldier. "Just in from the front lines. My commander ordered me to the throne room for R & R."

I relieved the soldier of his sword and shield and swept my arm toward the joyful scene in an invitation to join the celebration. As I placed the weapons near the door, I watched curiously while the soldier strode toward the center of the room. He seemed bewildered by the worship, unsure of how to proceed. I understood the feeling. He knew how to fight, but clearly, joy and song and dance were not part of his normal routine.

Awkwardly, he tried to sing. Compared to the beautiful tones filling the room, he sounded a bit like a rooster just learning to crow. The worse he sounded, the harder he tried and the harder he tried the worse he sounded. I suppressed a chuckle as the poor soldier's clamor intensified. Then he attempted to join in the dance. I was glad he had left his weapons at the door. Like an oversized puppy, he bumped into dancers and tripped over his own feet. With admirable determination, the soldier worked even harder, watching the dancers and trying to copy their moves. His awkward attempts to join in did not detract from the worship, but from what I could see, it hardly seemed restful or refreshing.

Quietly, Cap left his post and moved unhurriedly toward the soldier. Putting his hand firmly on the young man's shoulder, Cap whispered in his ear. Gradually, the soldier's shoulders relaxed, his frenzied eyes became peaceful; he looked toward the King and gave a deep sigh of relief.

Soon, all of his features began to soften. His breathing became natural and rhythmic. I braced myself for a bellow as he opened his mouth and began to sing. But, this time, the soldier's voice blended with the throne room's choir in a rich baritone. He swayed in time with the music and eventually began dancing in lovely, graceful movements. His eyes never left the King and his body never bumped or even touched the other dancers.

Cap returned to his post. Unable to hold my curiosity any longer, I slipped across the room to Cap's side and asked, "What did you say to him, Cap?"

"I simply said, 'Stop striving,' " Cap replied.

And He said,
"My presence shall go with thee,
and I will give thee rest."

EXODUS 33:14

# HARMONY

There were no footsteps on the path just now. Music continued quietly. My attention was drawn to two statesmen arguing their points before the King. As their heated exchange continued, the music faded, and I was able to hear their words.

"You are not wholly accurate, my esteemed colleague," declared one statesman. "You have mistaken the correct interpretation of the law. As a result, you are wrong in the precedent you are encouraging."

"I'm sure you have not listened to my case, sir," exclaimed the other debater. "If you had listened, you would have seen that I am absolutely correct in my interpretation, and if you would admit that I am right, we could institute this standard throughout the kingdom."

The argument continued, and as it did, the civility of the exchange deteriorated. Tension began to rise like a light fog in the throne room. The statesmen did not notice that the music had stopped. As one made a particularly powerful point, several soldiers in attendance dropped their swords and scrambled to pick them up. The other statesman's response caused several warriors to slump to the floor. Oblivious to the power-draining effect of their disagreement, the statesmen argued on. Rancor began to invade the debate, and the King, who had been calmly observing the two, lifted His scepter.

The opponents saw the scepter rise; their shock was obvious. They noticed the absence of worship, the reduced military might. Some visitors to the throne room even displayed a sickly pallor. What had happened? Realization dawned on each man simultaneously, and they knew they were somehow the cause of this uncomfortable, unhealthy stillness.

"We need a song," the King declared to the statesmen, obviously expecting them to provide one. Dumbfounded, they exchanged glances, and then each began a different song in a different key. Swords again fell to the ground and quiet groans could be heard from the gallery. The statesmen stopped. The King's steady gaze made it clear that a song was still required, so the two tried again. This time they sang the same song, in different keys, both belting out the melody with vigor but discord. Soldiers slumped, the statesmen's volume dwindled to silence, and they both appeared perplexed and embarrassed. The King, arms folded, lifted an eyebrow, and the two bowed in defeat and frustration.

Finally, after several uncomfortable moments of silence, the King allowed a grin to slip across His face. He began to sing the song beautifully, motioning for the statesmen to join in. Carried by the King's strong melody, the statesmen easily fell into lovely harmony. The result was a marvelous, powerful anthem. As the trio blended and crescendoed, warriors once again stood at attention, music accompanied the singers, and soon the throne room returned to full praise and power.

"Whew," I let out my breath in a relieved sigh and made a note to myself. "The kingdom is like a lovely song. Each singer may sing a different part, but when each part is in harmony with the other and following the melody of the King, the power and beauty is matchless."

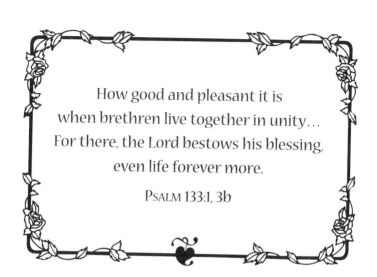

How good and pleasant it is
when brethren live together in unity…
For there, the Lord bestows his blessing,
even life forever more.

PSALM 133:1, 3b

# BROKEN

Lopsided, hesitant steps caught my ear—clump... schlumph...pause...clump... schlumph...pause—as if someone was stepping heavily with one foot and dragging the other behind. Anticipating another traveler's knock, I was poised to open the massive golden doors, but no knock came. Puzzled, I exchanged glances with Cap who raised his eyebrows and nodded toward the doors. Taking this as a suggestion to open them, I swung just one door ajar and glanced out.

There, standing with head down and arms limp at her side, was a young woman. I think she would have been lovely were it not for the bruises and gashes covering her face and arms. Her mangled left leg hung grotesquely, barely touching the ground. She began to sway, and as she slumped toward the floor, I threw open the door and caught her in my arms. Quickly, I turned, planning to carry her to the throne for healing, but as I took a step in that direction, she whispered, "No."

When I looked into her face, I saw shame and defeat. "Please," she begged, "let me just sit here against the wall." Knowing that a few moments face-to-face with the King Himself would transform her, I started to protest. A gesture from Cap convinced me to acquiesce to the young woman's pleadings, and as gently as I could, I set her down on a pillow along the wall near the grand doors.

Worship continued in the throne room. Statesmen came and went at the King's bidding. Pilgrims arrived with their requests. The music rose and fell. Beautiful fragrances filled the air. I continued to attend to my duties but kept watch over the poor woman who crouched like a wounded sparrow on her pillow by the wall. As the hours passed, I noticed her bruises fading and the deep gashes losing their angry redness. Even her mangled leg, though still scarred and crooked, seemed to "pink up" with a flow of life that had been absent before.

"Soon now," I thought. "Soon, she will rise and approach the King." The look of shame receded, replaced by wonder. She seemed to be enjoying herself.

Time went by, and then the young woman slowly rose to her feet—her shoulders straighter, her bearing more confident, her head held higher. I reached to help her up and lead her to the throne, but she moved past me in the opposite direction, and still limping, slipped out the door and back into the shadows along the path.

I was dismayed. What a loss! I looked to Cap

aghast. I had expected her to leave completely whole. I was sure she could have been fully restored if she had just approached the King. In fact, I was angry that she had turned away.

"Not all who come in are instantly made whole, my friend. She will be back," my patient mentor explained.

As had become my habit, I looked again to the throne. The King was at that very moment dispatching guardians who passed through the doors and headed down the path in the direction the young woman had disappeared.

A bruised reed he
will not break.

ISAIAH 42:3a

# UNLIKELY PILGRIM

Footsteps beckoned me toward the throne room's immense doors once again. But as I opened the doors and prepared to graciously usher the traveler in, I stopped short. My first instinct was to bar this particular traveler's way and refuse him entrance.

There, facing me, stood a man dressed in the leggings and tunic of the other realm—the enemy I had fought against so long and hard in my previous assignments. My training surged into action as I took in every aspect of the traveler's appearance. Finally, my examination reached the man's face. It was not like the faces I had confronted in battle. This man's face was serene and unguarded. There was no aggression, no threat in his manner.

Seeming to understand my reaction, the unlikely guest waited patiently as I fought my internal battle. Finally, I settled the matter, realizing this person had every right to approach the King and swung the doors wide in the best gesture of acceptance and welcome I could muster.

A relieved smile burst on the foreigner's face, and, to my astonishment, he hugged me before he passed through the doors to the King's presence. Still a little wary, I watched protectively as he approached the King. From where I stood, I could view the profile of this new arrival and was surprised to see tears streaming down the swarthy cheeks. As he drew near, he hesitated, but the King motioned him forward. Soon, the foreigner was engulfed in the King's welcoming embrace.

As time passed and the foreigner rose to leave, I

expected the King to provide him with a robe suitable for a citizen of the kingdom. But the King did nothing to change the newcomer's appearance. He embraced him again and whispered in the former warrior's ear, which caused a fresh cascade of tears. The King watched lovingly as the no-longer-foreigner left the throne room and headed down the path, not toward the cities of the King's realm, but toward the "other" realm.

As I thought about what I had just seen I remembered the King's words, "I am not willing that any should perish."

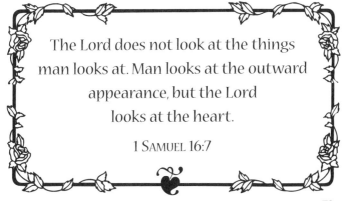

The Lord does not look at the things man looks at. Man looks at the outward appearance, but the Lord looks at the heart.

1 SAMUEL 16:7

# FAILURE

A sense of victory was spreading through the throne room. I loved these times. Maintaining the outward demeanor of a soldier, my heart would swell with the internal joy of the dance, the symphonic anthems, the palace guards in full regalia—the heartbeart of the throne room. The dull knock on the grand doors seemed unreal, out-of-place. Unsure I had heard it at all, I waited and listened. Moments passed. There it was again—thud, thud, thud—lifeless, but very much real.

By this time, I had learned not to guess what or who would be waiting on the other side of the doors; I simply swung them wide. To my surprise, the face I beheld was familiar. Standing there, eye-to-eye with me, was the captain under whom I had served for many years. Automatically raising my arm in salute, I noticed the determined effort it cost my former captain to raise his hand in the customary return gesture of respect. Alarmed, I examined his eyes for a clue and saw hollowness coupled with what could only be devastation.

Without words, the captain lowered his arm and proceeded toward the center of the throne room. My heart ached as I observed the sag in my former captain's once proud shoulders, the hesitation in his soldier's gait, the tremendous weariness pervading every movement. His uniform was in tatters. There was a gash on his cheek; he was limping and his right arm seemed to rest at an odd angle.

The anthems quieted as the captain continued slowly forward, and the King slipped quietly from His throne to meet him. Avoiding the King's eyes, tears moistening his cheeks, the captain solemnly laid his shield on the marble floor and removed his captain's braid from his shoulder, placing it at the King's feet. Using both hands, he slowly, laboriously drew his brilliant sword from its scabbard and very deliberately broke it against his thigh. This too was laid at the King's feet. Finally, removing his belt, the captain stripped off his armor and let it fall to the floor. Now, clothed only in a plain white tunic, he looked up to the King's crest. Still not meeting the King's eyes, the captain summoned his last vestige of strength to report, "My King, I have failed," and slumped to the floor.

I made a move to help the captain, but was restrained by a knowing hand. So I watched as the King focused on the fallen soldier—His face a study in compassion. He knelt before the man and placing His arms around his shoulders, rocked him as He would a child while the captain wept into the royal robe. When the sobs subsided, the King drew back slightly and firmly lifted the captain's face until he was compelled to meet the King's gaze. Minutes passed as the two remained face-to-face, eyes locked. The King's look of knowing acceptance was devoid of surprise or rejection. Eventually, the King gracefully rose with His hand still under captain's chin and their eyes locked.

When they were standing, the King said simply, "My child."

In a fluid motion, the King replaced the captain's armor, re-clasped the belt around the captain's middle, and wrapped the captain's hand around the shield once more. Bending, He reached for the captain's broken sword. The gallery gasped in wonder as the King drew the sword once more whole, sharp, and brilliant. With a flare, He offered it back to the captain. Wonder mingled with humility on the captain's face as he took the sword and with practiced grace sheathed it in a single stroke. The King put His arm around the captain's shoulders and without hesitation, began to outline his next assignment.

When the council was over, the captain rose to full stature, saluted the King, and turned to march back to his duties in the realm. However, just before he reached the grand doors, he turned and, for a time, simply joined in the worship mounting once again in the throne room.

When he turned and faced the doors, his eyes reflected the peace and strength of the King. We exchanged brisk salutes as he passed and the doors closed behind him as he returned to the work he'd been given.

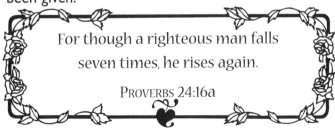

For though a righteous man falls seven times, he rises again.

PROVERBS 24:16a

# THE TRYST

As time went on, the flow of activity in the throne room became more familiar to me. I looked to Cap less for explanation. More often, now, we shared an understanding of the significance of a particular moment or event. I even began to anticipate the King's wishes.

From my first few hours in the throne room, I realized that, while many events were unique dramas to be played out only once, certain events occurred with absolute regularity. Such a moment was now approaching. I watched the King conclude a discussion he was having with a trusted general concerning affairs of state even while stealing a glance or two toward the doors. Soon, I knew I would hear confident, eager footsteps on the path and, as I opened the door, I knew that behind me, the King would be moving toward the less formal sitting area.

There were the footsteps now. As I swung open the massive doors, I smiled down at the slightly built guest as she entered. She greeted me with her usual kind word of appreciation and beautiful smile, then turned her full attention to the place she came every day to meet her King. As she crossed the great hall, her feet manifested her anticipation in a little, joyful dance. The King, aglow Himself with welcome and delight, moved to meet her, and they danced their way together to the sitting area.

Tea had been laid, and as they shared the refreshment, the King's pleasure in her animated conversation was obvious. Sometimes, their conversations were quite serious, sometimes passionate. Today, however, the petite guest was simply listening as the King spoke quietly, earnestly, of matters that were vitally important to Him. Occasionally, she would ask a pertinent question, but mostly, she listened with complete concentration. At these times, I noticed, the King's voice became its most melodious and His demeanor totally relaxed.

The traveler came daily to the "trysting" time, simply to be with the King—to be there for the King. During these times, I had never seen her make requests for the King's aid or even seek His approval. She came only to bring the King her gift, and it was clear that the gift she brought to the King was herself.

My beloved spoke, and said unto me,
"Rise up, my love, my fair one, and come away."

SONG OF SOLOMON 2:10 (KJV)

# FRONT AND CENTER

What a day! All my dreams concerning a post in the throne room were realized and surpassed. I was standing comfortably at my post enjoying a happy reverie reviewing the day's events, while remaining alert to the sounds outside the doors and ready to respond to Cap's instructions. From my post, I vicariously enjoyed the experiences of each fellow traveler to whom I opened the doors.

"Doorkeeper," the King's commanding voice jarred me to attention. "Front and center." Panic struck the pit of my stomach. I'm sure my eyes were the size of my shield, the blood left my face, my knees began to knock and my heart was pounding so hard surely it was visible through my tunic. I turned toward the throne.

I maintained my soldier's bearing (albeit a little wobbly) and marched to position front and center to the King. Even in the midst of flustered emotions, I was moved by the King's presence as I bowed before Him. Peace overcame the panic as I looked up.

A strong hand on my shoulder sent warmth through my entire body and with it came absolute calm. Looking at the hand on my shoulder, I followed the royal lines of the sleeve up the arm to the shoulder and finally the face of my King Himself. Immediately, everything ceased to exist for me except the King. Love, acceptance, and approval engulfed me as the King's presence began to permeate my being. My heart seemed to rise to eye level. I knew I was not just seeing the King's eyes; I was experiencing the King's heart.

Then the King spoke, "Enter in, my good and faithful servant." And He pulled me into His arms in a tremendous hug and I...soared. No longer enjoying the worship, I was the worship. Fearlessly, freely, I danced and sang and worshipped and released all of the love that had grown inside me through my years in the King's service. I was consumed with my King, utterly oblivious to clapping and delight around me. All I saw was my King. All I wanted was my King. All I knew was my King. And, my life was complete.

Well done, good and faithful servant...
come and share our master's happiness.

MATTHEW 25:2b,d

# CROWNS

Something was changing in the throne room. This was a day like no other. The intensity of worship, the growing cadre of warriors with none being dispatched, the feeling of anticipation from the gallery—it was all reaching a feverish pitch. What was happening? I looked at Cap, who said simply, "We will see."

Now, an anthem was commencing—quietly at first, flutes and strings beginning the theme. Then the trumpets and horns joined in. Soon the full throne-room symphony resounded. The music was riveting—commanding. Voices were added, all singing this song, a song I had never heard before. The harmony was amazing creating a power unlike anything I had ever experienced. What was happening?

The question went unanswered, yet I was not afraid. I experienced only a prevailing sense of awe and anticipation.

Those in the gallery stepped from their places and moved toward the center of the hall. As each, one at a time, set foot on the marble, their face shone, their clothing became a luminescent white robe, and a golden crown appeared on their head. They began to dance. In graceful, flowing movements, they embodied their worship.

I stood transfixed until I heard footsteps on the path—many, many footsteps! I swung the grand doors open wide; my heart lurched. The path was completely overrun, filled as far as my eyes could see. From every corner of the realm, they came, citizens of the kingdom. Hundreds, thousands of the faces were familiar. They had passed through these doors before, but today things were clearly different. Today, they were walking in cadence with the anthem; in fact, as they walked, they were singing with the throne-room choir.

I began to distinguish faces. There, at the front, of course, was the King's little daughter dancing her way toward the throne room hand-in-hand with a friend. Ah, there was the wounded woman, no longer limping, keeping pace with the crowd. Behind her I could see—could it be?—Yes! It was my old captain, sword at his side, royal uniform in top shape. He was striding joyfully, arm-in-arm with the no-longer-lost son. Here came Deeter, shuffling happily, her eyes proving she certainly knew what was coming next. They were all there—every one whom I had helped through the great doors.

As each stepped through the doors this last time, they were transformed just as the members of the gallery had been, and each began to dance as they joined in the anthem's chorus, "Worthy, worthy, worthy."

Time stopped, but the procession continued. In what seemed like only a moment, everyone was fully assembled in the throne room. No one remained outside on the path. Cap and I reached one more time to shut the magnificent golden doors. Together, we turned to the throne and, stepping onto the marble floor, were transformed and became part of the flowing, worshipping throng.

A drum-roll sounded and suddenly all was silent. Then we heard the words we had waited eons to hear. "Behold the Lamb." All eyes turned to the throne and the sight that met us there was indescribable. Before us, was the Lamb—the King, Jesus, He Who is Love, He Who is Holy. What words can describe such a sight?

As one, we fell down before Him, and then, one-by-one, rose and came face-to-face with the Lamb. In the presence of His love and holiness, each one took off their crown and threw it down at His feet. My turn came, and as the adoration in my heart reached my feet, I fairly floated to face the Lamb. There, before Him, I knew I needed no other reward than to be in the Lamb's presence, and with a liberating dance of joy and abandonment, I cast my crown among the many at the feet of the Lamb. And so…eternity began.

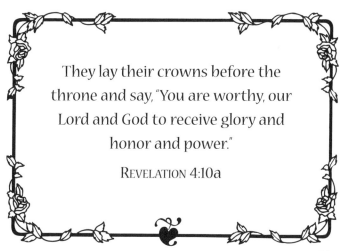

They lay their crowns before the throne and say, "You are worthy, our Lord and God to receive glory and honor and power."

REVELATION 4:10a

# Epilogue: A Royal Invitation

For every human being, life is a journey. We enter life on our way to eternity. We visit many ports of call: childhood, adolescence, parenthood, success, failure, happiness, depression, birth and death. We search desperately for our place in this world. Where do we belong? Where do we fit in?

I extend to you an invitation to the one port of call where I know you belong—to the one place in all existence where you are always welcome and wanted. Come to the throne room. Knock and the King Himself will open the door for you. Simply say, "Here I am, show me the way." And He will.

Oh taste and see that the Lord is good.
Blessed is the man [or woman]
who trusts in Him.

PSALM 34:8